MARILYN

THE STAR AND HER MUSIC

JG
PRESS

Credits

Published by World Publications Group, Inc.
140 Laurel Street
East Bridgewater, MA 02333
www.wrldpub.com

PAGE 1: Marilyn poses on a Singer automobile
on the set of the romantic comedy *How to Marry
a Millionaire* that was released in 1953.

LEFT: Marilyn was desperate to be regarded as
an actor rather than a sexpot and worked with
Lee Strasberg at the Actors Studio from 1955.

Contents

Introduction

In 1998 Marilyn Monroe was voted *Playboy* magazine's "Sexiest Female Star of the Twentieth Century." Some may argue with such an accolade, but many millions would agree.

It's just one of hundreds of plaudits that have been awarded to Marilyn during the, almost, fifty years since her tragic death. A year after the *Playboy* award, in an auction of Marilyn's personal effects at Christie's in New York at what was called "The Sale of the Century," millions of dollars were spent by collectors all eager to own a piece of her. Around the world there are more Marilyn Monroe impersonators than of any other celebrity. Her movies are watched on DVD, TV, and cable channels in just about every country on earth and there are more tribute sites on the web to her than any other actress—alive or dead. There have been numerous books written about her 36 years on earth; all try to make sense of her appeal while trying to make sense of her life.

The enduring fascination with Marilyn can, in part, be put down to the fact that no one has ever quite understood her. She managed to be a little girl lost, while at the same time being outrageously sexy. She was vulnerable, yet she flaunted her body. At times she craved acceptance as an actress, yet in her last, unfinished, movie she took her clothes off—happy to appear naked. Was she a great actress or was she just stumbling through, just being herself? According to Sir Laurence Olivier, one of her co-stars and a great actor himself, "She is a brilliant comedienne, which to me means she also is an extremely skilled actress."

Marilyn lived the majority of her life on the outside. As a child she was unwanted by a mother who spent much of her life in a psychiatric hospital; accordingly, Marilyn was never even sure who her father was. Married three times, she was unable to be what her husbands wanted her to be. They had been attracted by what they saw and then wanted to change her into something she was incapable of being. She never found the kind of happiness with a man that she dreamed of, yet she never behaved in a way that would allow a man to completely trust in her.

OPPOSITE: Marilyn on her patio at home in Brentwood, California in May 1953.

Hollywood was also attracted to what they saw, they tried to make her be something that they could manage and manipulate into making them money. Marilyn was never happy with that and at times fought against it, with the result that she was never really accepted by Hollywood. She was a natural talent who constantly tried to be something different. She was also hurt by Hollywood; she blamed them for her problems. Marilyn was no different to the rest of us; it's often easier to blame others.

Marilyn's last interview with a *Life* magazine journalist is heartbreaking. You hear a woman who is at times unsure, at times sad, at times clearly grasping for the strands of reality. What you also hear is nothing like the "little girl lost voice" that she so often adopted as her public persona. She also revealed that she would love to have been like a normal person—a cleaning woman. Being allowed to do the things that ordinary people do without having to be "Marilyn Monroe." Once she said goodbye to Norma Jeane the chances of ever having what passes for a normal life were lost forever. Above all else, Marilyn does not sound entirely sober. Whether it was drink or drugs, who can say, but many years earlier Marilyn had set off down the complete opposite of the mythical yellow brick road. Sometimes people do not decide these things, they just happen

Yet despite her human frailties, her failings, and her problems Marilyn's memory is cherished by millions of people the world over. Ever since her death, at a comparatively young age, there have been countless conspiracy theories; theories that have prevented some from remembering how she was a talented, yet fragile, actress. From "poor little orphan girl" to a worldwide celebrity, this is the story of how Norma Jeane became Marilyn Monroe and captured the imagination of the world.

"If I am a star, the people made me a star"

Marilyn Monroe in her
last interview

LEFT: U.S. Postmaster General Marvin Runyon and Anna Strasberg unveil the postage stamp commemorating Marilyn.

OPPOSITE: Vivacious, beautiful, a star in the making. The black and white photograph does no justice to the spectacular Oleg Cassini red velvet sheath gown in which Marilyn received her Henrietta on January 26, 1952.

The Early Years
1926–1950

On June 1, 1926, a baby that her mother would name Norma Jeane was born in a charity ward of a Los Angeles hospital. It would be the start of a journey through life that would see the girl go from being unwanted by anyone to wanted by everyone.

Marilyn Monroe, like just about every actress of her generation, and many others besides, had a different birth name. The name on her birth certificate is Norma Jeane Mortenson; but like so much of what passes for the facts that surround the life of one of the movies' most legendary actresses it's not remotely true. Ask most people to give Marilyn's real name and they can usually come up with Norma Jeane, thanks to Elton John's ode to Monroe, "Candle in the Wind." Some will be able to tell you her surname was, for a while, Baker, which is also true, for Marilyn was baptized Norma Jeane Baker.

Marilyn's mother was born Gladys Pearl Monroe in May 1902 to Della Mae and Otis Elmer Monroe. By the time Gladys was 11 years old her mother and brother Marion had moved to Venice, an area of Los Angeles that sits next to the Pacific Ocean. She started hanging out at the pier in Venice where, two years later, she met 26-year-old Jasper Newton "Jap" Baker. Ten days before her 15th birthday Gladys Pearl Monroe married the man of her dreams.

Gladys quickly had two babies—Robert Kermit (more often called Jack) and in 1919 a girl she named Bernice Inez. They all lived with Della and her new boyfriend on Coral Canal in Venice. Within two years Gladys Baker, as she now was, sought a divorce as well as claiming she was not really cut out to be a mother. This went through in May 1922, and Baker ended up with the children in Kentucky.

Gladys moved to Hollywood, to take up a job in the fledgling movie business as a cutter and splicer at Consolidated Film Industries. Soon she met a 27-year-old man named Martin Edward Mortensen, who was a gas fitter for the Los Angeles Gas and Electric Company. On October 11, 1924, 22-year-old Gladys married Mortensen in

OPPOSITE: Gladys divorced Edward Mortenson on June 1, 1927. This photo, taken around 1929, shows Norma Jeane (below right) and her mother Gladys Baker (above right) with sister-in-law Olyve and her daughter Ida Mae.

ABOVE and OPPOSITE: In 1928 Norma Jeane, Gladys, her brother Marion, his wife Olyve, and their daughter Ida Mae went to the beach with friends.

Hollywood. Within six months, Gladys went back to calling herself Baker and it was at this point that she discovered she was pregnant. Unsure of who the father was Gladys gave birth to a baby girl at 9:30am on June 1, 1926, at Los Angeles County Medical Center in Boyle Heights. Gladys stated that Norma Jeane was her third child but the only one to still be living. There has been conjecture ever since as to who Marilyn Monroe's father might be. The fact that it says "Mortenson" on her birth certificate is inconclusive, of course. In the 1950s Marilyn wrote an autobiography with Ben Hecht, the American screenwriter, director, producer, playwright, and novelist. In it she talks of being shown a photograph of a man with a small "Clark Gable-like" moustache that her mother said was her father—she also said that he was killed in an auto wreck in New York City.

At first Norma Jeane was brought up by neighbors of her grandmother, Della. Gladys paid Ida and Albert Bolander $25 a month to look after Norma Jeane. But in summer 1933 she went to live with her mother in a three-bedroom bungalow close to the Hollywood Bowl. It seems that for a while Gladys and Norma Jeane shared what passed for a normal life. They would visit Hollywood Boulevard and do what most mothers and daughters do. Everything was fine until Grace lost her job. It was sometime after this that Gladys was taken to Metropolitan State Hospital in Norwalk. She was there in January 1935 and was diagnosed with paranoid schizophrenia. Norma Jeane was never to live with her mother again; she was not yet nine years old.

Marilyn went to live with her mother's friend Grace McKee—a much happier existence for Norma Jeane. Grace, as well as working in the movie business, loved the glamour and the romance of the cinema and filled her friend's daughter's head with stories of the movie greats. She would take Norma Jeane down to Grauman's Chinese Theatre where she encouraged her to put her hands in the hand imprints in the concrete, in particular Jean Harlow's. Norma Jeane collected pictures cut from movie magazines, and while it's easy to link that with who and what she became, so did hundreds of thousands of girls across America and around the world.

Her neighbors while she was living with Grace were the Dougherty family whose son, 20-year-old Jim, worked in the aviation industry.

Jim married Norma Jeane on June 19, 1942, at the home of an attorney friend of Grace and her husband; she had just had her 16th birthday. They seem to have been happy together initially, and by February 1944 they were living on Catalina Island where Jim was undergoing training following his call-up into the merchant marine.

After Jim went to sea, Marilyn moved back to Los Angeles to live with his parents. While Jim was away she learned to drive and, most importantly, got a job. Like many American women, Norma Jeane worked to support the war effort. She found employment at the Radio Plane Company; they made radio-controlled pilotless aircraft that were used for target practice.

Women working on the home front often attracted photographers keen to portray how the war had changed things so much for them, especially if they worked in unfamiliar roles. If a women was pretty so much the better, which is exactly what the Army photographer who arrived at the Radio Plane Company thought when he saw Norma Jeane. His name was David Conover, and before the war he had had a studio on Sunset Boulevard. Soon he was getting Norma Jeane to pose away from the factory environment.

Conover showed the pictures to another photographer, and it was following this that Norma Jeane was introduced to Emmeline Snivley, the owner of the Blue Book Modeling Agency. That was the moment when everything changed.

By early 1945, with Jim Dougherty still at sea, Norma Jeane had left her in-laws' house; she stayed

"All those guys chasing after her, taking pictures of her. I wanted her to be a wife... I wanted a normal life. She didn't."

Jim Dougherty

briefly with a relative before living at the Hollywood Studio Club. In the meantime, she had lightened her hair considerably on the advice of another photographer she worked for. It was on June 26, 1946, that Norma Jeane appeared on the cover of *Yank* magazine, photographed by David Conover; by the end of the year, she and Dougherty were divorced. Like many other stars, Marilyn trod the tried and tested path from model to the movies. Her success as a model came at the cost of her marriage to Jim Dougherty.

The now-single Norma Jeane shared a room with another aspirant at the Hollywood Studio Club, and according to that girl she was posing in some of the more risqué magazines, which in itself was risky for Norma Jeane's ambitions. It could have prevented her from getting straight modeling work, but such was the camera's love for her that she found herself working constantly. She worked with photographer Andre de Dienes, who took a series of shots of her during a month-long trip to Washington State at Christmas 1945 and sold the images worldwide. On April 13, 1946, she appeared as a flower picker on the cover of a British magazine called *Leader*. This was before her first-ever cover shot on America's *Family Circle* magazine.

Within a month of making the cover of *Yank* magazine, Norma Jeane had her first serious opportunity to make the move from modeling to movies. When precisely she decided that this was what she wanted to do is unclear; her own version of her life in those pre-fame years is as much fiction as fact.

In order to get a divorce from Jim Dougherty, Norma Jeane spent six weeks in Las Vegas to secure the necessary residential qualifications to complete it quickly. It was on her return that she had a meeting with Ben Lyon, on July 17, 1946, at 20th Century-Fox; the 45-year-old Lyon had been an actor and was now an executive at the studio. She was naturally nervous and, according to Lyon, answered his questions with a "forthright honesty." Impressed by Norma Jeane's openness, Lyon decided to do a screen test with her. Two days later, she was back at 20th Century-Fox where they took some silent color footage of her walking, sitting, and moving in and out of shot. The cameraman that day was Leon Shamroy, who would later film her in *There's no Business like Showbusiness*.

Ben Lyon was impressed with what he saw. He liked the fact that she seemed unconsciously to combine innocence and an allure, bordering on out-and-out sex. He immediately arranged to show her screen test to Darryl F. Zanuck, the man who had founded Twentieth Century Pictures in 1933 before buying out Fox Studios to become 20th Century-Fox. Zanuck was less than impressed. He considered her just another pretty model who was not really worth wasting their time on. Lyon was convinced otherwise and he persisted, and eventually Zanuck relented, agreeing to let his Head of New Talent have his way.

Norma Jeane initially signed a minimum contract with Lyon, who paid her $75 per week—she had her foot on the first rung of the movie ladder. She signed her contract at the end of August, two weeks before her divorce to Jim Dougherty was finalized.

For the purposes of her contract with 20th Century-Fox, Norma Jeane was no longer Norma Jeane Baker. In *My Story* Marilyn tells an elaborate tale about her aunt telling her, for the first time, that her grandmother's name was Monroe and how she was related

OPPOSITE: Norma Jean's screen test—in one of the least flattering outfits imaginable.

to the fifth president of the United States, James Monroe. According to Norma Jeane's aunt Grace, Gladys was, "directly descended" from the early-19th-century president.

The precise truth about how Norma Jeane became Marilyn Monroe we'll probably never know. Alliteration certainly can work really well, and as we all now feel so comfortable with the notion of Marilyn Monroe it sounds just perfect. It's likely that Ben Lyon had a hand in it, probably with a little help from his protégé. However, it was no instant decision; for a little while Lyon called her Carole Lind, but this did not last. Almost immediately after signing for Fox, Marilyn got her first part—in *The Shocking Miss Pilgrim*—although it was a very small one that would go unnoticed because she went uncredited when the movie was released in early 1947.

Read virtually any biography of Marilyn Monroe and it will tell you that her first speaking role was in a movie called *Scudda Hoo! Scudda Hay!* Now it is just possible that Marilyn made this film before she made *Dangerous Years*, but the latter movie was released first. *Dangerous Years* provided Marilyn with just a single day's work, although as a contract actor she got paid whether she was on set or not.

OPPOSITE: Norma Jeane Dougherty, a beautiful 19-year-old, photographed by William Carroll in Castle Rock State Park, CA.

BELOW: Norma Jeane got a job at Radio Plane Munitions Factory. She is seen with some of her fellow workers at a picnic in Balboa Park, San Diego, CA.

Throughout this period Marilyn also took acting lessons, paid for by 20th Century-Fox, at the Actors' Lab behind Schwab's drugstore on Sunset Boulevard; from all available reports it appears she did not show huge promise during these lessons. Marilyn's last movie, at least in terms of its release, while under contract to 20th Century-Fox is another attempt to make "agriculture pay," as Bosley Crowther from *The New York Times* succinctly summed it all up. Called *Green Grass of Wyoming*, Marilyn's involvement was uncredited: she appears as a square-dancer in this tale of humans and animals on a ranch.

And then Marilyn was fired—sacked as a contract actor for 20th Century-Fox in what are confusing and conflicting circumstances. The company had spent somewhere between $4,000 and $6,500 on her during the year she was under contract; that's anything up to $100,000 in today's money. What did they get for that? Three uncredited roles in which the most she said was, "hello," and possibly not even that, and two movies in which she featured for under 30 seconds of dialogue in total. That would have been fine if it had been all about Marilyn serving an apprenticeship, but at the time few had any confidence in her ability to make it beyond being a pretty face in the background— just a bit-part actor who would not even warrant a footnote in movie history.

According to Marilyn, Darryl F. Zanuck thought she might turn into an actress one day, but "your type of looks is definitely against you." This appears to be the basis on which she was fired from her contract. Not even Marilyn's friendship with Joe Schenk, the 70-year-old who was the absolute head of 20th Century-Fox, could save her. Ben Lyon certainly seems to have been genuinely surprised that it happened.

However, Marilyn had Joe Schenk to thank for helping her to land her next job. He put in that all-important call to Harry Cohn at Columbia Pictures and asked him to give her a six-month contact. Harry obliged and Marilyn was back under contract from March 1948, once again on a minimum weekly wage of $75. She was also back living at the Hollywood Studio Club after a time spent in her own apartment.

After working with one of Columbia Pictures' drama teachers Marilyn got her first break with her new studio. It was a role that not only required her to speak but also to sing. This necessitated some extra lessons that the studio arranged for her to get from Fred Karger, Columbia's Director of Music. It was an uphill task because Marilyn was far from a natural. Her biggest problem was not her voice but the fact that she was incredibly nervous about singing in front of people.

Ladies of the Chorus was released in February 1949, after Marilyn's contract with Columbia had been terminated in the fall. But at about the same time as *Ladies of the Chorus* came out Marilyn got a part in another film, although her appearance was in a minor role. *Love Happy* is a Marx Brothers movie and they had a particular requirement. "Someone I met at a lunch counter told me they were making retakes and needed a girl for a bit part." When she went on set Groucho said to her, "This role calls for a young lady who can walk by me in such a manner as it arouses my elderly libido and causes smoke to come from my ears." Groucho had found the perfect girl.

Not only was Marilyn in the movie but also she was used by United Artists to promote the film. She went to New York, her first trip to Manhattan, where she did some

BELOW: Marilyn's first significant role in movies was in her only Columbia movie: *Ladies Of The Chorus*.

ABOVE and ABOVE RIGHT: Marilyn was only on screen for a short time in *Love Happy*—some thirty-nine seconds, but it got her noticed.

OPPOSITE: At some stage in 1949 Marilyn met Johnny Hyde, vice president of William Morris, who fell for her. He got her to lighten her hair and took over as her agent.

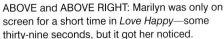

photo assignments as well as going to some of the Big Apple's bigger nightspots. All too quickly New York was over, and she headed to the Midwest to carry on promoting *Love Happy* before heading home to Los Angeles and an event that would change the course of her career.

Not long after Marilyn came back from her promotional trip, she went to a party in Palm Springs thrown by Hollywood producer Sam Spiegel where she met Johnny Hyde, an agent with the William Morris Agency. Hyde was one of those Hollywood behind-the-scenes men who wielded incredible power and influence. Hyde, in his early fifties, was smitten by Marilyn and, despite being ill with a heart problem, he took her on as a client. He had made his name representing Esther Williams, Lana Turner, and also Bob Hope, who he resembled facially.

Hyde housed Marilyn in a hotel, and through his influence he got her a part, albeit a small one, in a 20th Century-Fox Western called *A Ticket to Tomahawk*. Hyde got Marilyn to lighten her hair to create her signature peroxide blonde look and, most importantly, to keep it that way. He also encouraged her to have some minor plastic surgery on her chin to deal with some blemishes, although not her nose, as has been claimed.

Learning The Ropes
1950–1952

Like many other stars, Marilyn trod the tried and tested path from model to the movies. However, for every one that makes it hundreds are left behind, and Marilyn was no overnight sensation.

> *"She hardly had to open her mouth and I knew she was right for the part. She was exceptional."*
>
> John Huston

Around the end of 1949 and the early part of 1950, Marilyn was living with John Carroll and his wife Lucille Ryman; she worked for MGM and it was the Carrolls that took Marilyn to Sam Spiegel's party in Palm Springs. They had a soft spot for Marilyn and were keen to help her in whatever ways they could. This connection proved invaluable when Lucille and Hyde engineered a small role for Marilyn in *The Asphalt Jungle*, a movie directed by John Huston. Before her audition with Huston, Marilyn was extremely nervous. Anxious to please Hyde and the Carrolls, she really worked hard to present herself properly. In the event she had no real reason to worry, Huston was bowled over by her talent.

Shooting began on *The Asphalt Jungle* as soon as *A Ticket to Tomahawk* had finished; it was the start of Marilyn's busiest year, so far, in Hollywood. *The Asphalt Jungle* was released in late May and according to *The New York Times*, "Mr. Huston has filmed a straight crime story about as cleverly and graphically as it could be filmed."

Before 1950 was over, Marilyn worked on three more movies, all of which came out within a week of one another in October. There was another, called *Right Cross*, for MGM in which she had a small, uncredited, part; then, *Fireball*, a low-budget black-and-white movie about a roller derby star, and finally a small part in *All About Eve*.

Then in December, Johnny Hyde, the one man who had been unequivocally good and caring towards Marilyn, died in Cedars of Lebanon Hospital on Fountain Avenue, Los Angeles. It was a tragic end to a year in which Marilyn had seemed to turn something of a Hollywood corner. Yet it could all so easily be taking her down a road to nowhere without her mentor and guide.

The loss of Johnny Hyde from Marilyn's life was a devastating blow. She had signed a short contract with 20th Century-Fox in mid-December, one that had been arranged by Johnny Hyde, but it did not bode well for her that the head of the studio thought her dumb.

OPPOSITE: Marilyn was cast as a showgirl in *A Ticket to Tomahawk* and sang "Oh, What A Forward Young Man You Are."

The new Fox picture in which Marilyn had a small part was *As Young as You Feel*, which starred Monty Woolley and Thelma Ritter. It was a long way from the type of role that Marilyn wanted to play, but it did bring her into contact with a man who would play a significant role in her life. Elia Kazan, who was working on his movie adaptation of Tennessee Williams' *A Street Car Named Desire*, came to the set of *As Young as You Feel* to see Harmon Jones, its director, who had edited Kazan's *Panic on the Streets* a couple of years earlier. Jones had told Kazan about Marilyn.

Accompanying Kazan that day was Arthur Miller, a playwright, communist sympathizer, journalist, and friend of the Hollywood director. Miller was a brilliant writer whose *Death of a Salesman* had been directed by Kazan on Broadway two years earlier; the intellectual Miller was smitten with Marilyn from the moment he laid eyes on her. The only problem was that he had been married for ten years to his childhood sweetheart. Marilyn was equally attracted to Miller, and they met again less than a week later at a party at the home of Charles Feldman of Famous Artists Agency. All too quickly Miller went back to living in New York with his wife and Marilyn went back to work on her latest minor movie role.

One day in early 1951, Marilyn drove herself to Famous Artists Agency office in Hollywood in her Pontiac convertible to meet with Hugh French. He told her he was having little or no luck in extending her contract with 20th Century-Fox. He did however have some good news in that she had been invited to the Fox's Exhibitors' party. It was an event when they brought in movie-theater owners from all across America to meet and greet their finest talent.

Marilyn arrived late for the party a few days later and made what can only be described as—an entrance. "Amid a slowly gathering hush, she stood there, a blonde apparition in a strapless cocktail gown, a little breathless as if she were Cinderella, just stepped from the pumpkin coach." It goes unrecorded what Susan Hayward, June Haver, Tyrone Power, Gregory Peck, and the real Fox stars had to say, but Marilyn was immediately escorted to the table of the President of 20th Century-Fox.

It was around this same time that Marilyn was asked to be one of the presenters for the Academy Awards at the RKO Pantages Theater on Hollywood and Vine. By May, and partly as a result of all this activity, French had landed a seven-year contract for Marilyn with 20th Century-Fox.

After a loan to MGM and a minor role, Marilyn's next important picture was to be *Love Nest*; it's another movie featuring one of Fox's regular stars, June Haver, with whom Marilyn had worked before. It was to be another minor role, although bigger than she had been used to—and at least for this movie Marilyn appeared in the movie-theater trailer which shows that Fox were at last alive to her cinematic pulling power.

Love Nest began showing in movie theaters in the middle of October 1951 and was followed two weeks later by the Los Angeles premier of *Let's Make it Legal*, Marilyn's fourth movie of 1951. The timing was perfect as it followed one of the first full-length articles about Marilyn to appear in a national magazine. Prior to this it had mostly been mentions in *Variety*, the trade magazine, movie reviews, and the Hollywood gossip

"Young Marilyn Monroe, who has logged less than fifty-minutes screen time, stole the show."

Collier's magazine

OPPOSITE: In 1990 *All About Eve* was one of the first fifty movies to be registered by the Library of Congress for preservation.

"A forceful actress, a gifted new star."

New York World Telegram

OPPOSITE: Marilyn wore a memorable polka dot bikini in *Love Nest* ... too good an opportunity to miss for Earl Theisen who took a series of pictures of her at the Beverly Carlton Hotel.

columns, although she did make the cover of a smaller magazine called *True Experiences*. *Collier's* magazine called their story in September "Hollywood's 1951 Model Blonde."

Photoplay magazine voted Marilyn "Hollywood's most promising star" in 1952, but, just five days after the new year had begun Marilyn's world was in danger of crashing down around her. Word of Marilyn posing nude for a calendar photo shoot two years earlier was beginning to leak out and 20th Century-Fox were concerned about how best to play it—the options were either to drop their promising star or they could use the publicity to their advantage.

Fox had already loaned Marilyn to RKO Pictures to make Fritz Lang's *Clash by Night*. She began work on the movie as her rush of 1951 releases were beginning to get general release across America. Marilyn benefited from what *Life* magazine described as her "best role since *The Asphalt Jungle*." Fox did the obvious and chose to stick with Marilyn and when the story of her modeling finally broke in early March, for a while the world went nuts for nude Marilyn pictures. Far from damaging her reputation it just upped her collateral to the point where it wouldn't be long before she went from being at the bottom of the list of credited actors on movie posters to the top of the list. As the old saying goes, there's no such thing as bad publicity just as long as they spell your name right.

In the wake of her loan out to RKO Marilyn was back at 20th Century-Fox for the first of four pictures she would make with the studio before 1952 was over. These releases all came out in what can only be described as a rush. All five movies had their premieres within a less than three-month period, starting with *Clash by Night* on June 16 and culminating with *Monkey Business* on September 5.

Marilyn, who had just celebrated her 26th birthday, had also met her future husband a few weeks earlier at a dinner date at the Villa Nova restaurant on Sunset Strip. It was a date she almost didn't keep because she had been told he was a baseball star and she felt she would have little to say to such a man. She felt he would probably be brash, boring, and possibly worse; in the event, when Marilyn was introduced to Joe DiMaggio she was surprised. Joe got Marilyn's phone number and shortly afterwards the two of them had dinner, alone and together.

Marilyn saw Elia Kazan shortly after her second "date" with Joe DiMaggio and told him all about it. Back home in Connecticut, Kazan met with his friend Arthur Miller and told him the news.

The first of Marilyn's three movies to be released in what remained of 1952 was *Don't Bother to Knock*, which had its premiere a week after *We're Not Married*. Marilyn had worked on her new movie prior to all the fuss around the nude calendar. Zanuck's view that Marilyn was ready for a better role was made easier by the fact that her role in *Don't Bother to Knock* required her to play a disturbed blonde.

The experience of working with Roy Ward Baker on *Don't Bother to Knock* was far from a happy one. Perhaps it was the pressure on Marilyn to perform in her first starring role, then again as it was his first Hollywood movie Baker was under some pressure as well. What was worrying the studio executives at Fox was the fact that Marilyn was

growing ever more popular, not at all hindered by the nude photo shoot, and yet she was not the kind of actress that other actors seemed to enjoy working with, nor was anyone at Fox particularly impressed with her intelligence or her personality. Zanuck grew increasingly frustrated and added to his dumb blonde remarks by calling her a "sexpot."

He was insistent that the studio give her no more dramatic roles. All he, and many others, thought she was good for was wiggling and walking. *O. Henry's Full House* was therefore just perfect, in the opinion of many of those in charge at Fox.

Marilyn's final movie to be released in 1952 was *Monkey Business*, the movie she was working on when she had her blind date with Joe DiMaggio. By the time the film was in cinemas right across America the newspapers had marriage right across the front pages, the publicity couldn't have been better.

While Marilyn worked on *Monkey Business* DiMaggio visited the studio, which was too good an opportunity for the PR people to miss out on. Cary Grant posed with Marilyn and DiMaggio, but when the photograph was released by 20th Century-Fox they had carefully edited Grant out of the shot, leaving the impression that it was just the two of them.

"She's a sexpot who wiggles and walks and breathes sex."

Darryl F. Zanuck

RIGHT: Barnaby and Edwina Fulton (Cary Grant and Ginger Rogers) bicker in *Monkey Business*. Barnaby's secretary Lois Laurel (Marilyn) watches on.

OPPOSITE: Joe DiMaggio visited the set of *Monkey Business* on the last day of shooting in April. Marilyn and he had been dating for some weeks and he was obviously very taken with her.

Movie Star
1953–1956

1953 was the year that Marilyn went from being a pin-up, a starlet, and a Hollywood hopeful, to fully-fledged movie star. *Gentlemen Prefer Blondes* was her first home run, and six months after its premiere in January 1954 she became Mrs. Joe DiMaggio and had her first real home.

"That's the way they think of me, with my skirt over my head."

Marilyn, June 1955

OPPOSITE: Marilyn shows off one of her form-fitting costumes for *Niagara*. The movie grossed $6 million and proved she was box office dynamite.

Marilyn's first movie of 1953 was *Niagara*, which had its premiere in New York City in late January. She had started work on it at the end of May 1952. From California she flew to meet up with DiMaggio in New York, where the couple spent a lot of time hanging out at one of Frank Sinatra's favorite Big Apple spots—Toots Shor's saloon and restaurant, right across from Madison Square Garden. Toots Shor's was the ultimate New York sports bar and a home-from-home for DiMaggio. There DiMaggio and Marilyn were a golden couple, even if at this point Marilyn was a rung or two down the celebrity ladder from Joe.

The story goes that Marilyn was told about the movie she was to star in after *Niagara* as she celebrated her 26th birthday. Howard Hawks, with whom she had worked on *Monkey Business*, argued with Zanuck that Marilyn was perfect for light comedy. Hawks was slated to direct *Gentlemen Prefer Blondes* and as it called for its star to sing and dance Zanuck was convinced Marilyn was not up to it—however Hawks finally persuaded him that Marilyn could do it.

Work began in November 1952; besides the usual pre-production work, Marilyn was also put through her paces by Jack Cole, a Fox stalwart, who had been tasked with choreographing the movie's dance sequences. While not only having singing lessons but also learning some reasonably difficult dance routines—for an untrained dancer—Marilyn found it all very arduous. New skills, when added to the burden of being the movie's star, appear to have brought on a bad attack of nerves for Marilyn. So much so that she would constantly arrive late on set, which in turn, frustrated Howard Hawks who considered her unprofessional.

Much to everyone's surprise, Marilyn got along really well with Jane Russell. Through the course of their conversations Russell realized that Marilyn constantly arriving late on set had nothing to do with poor timekeeping and everything to do with her nerves. Her stage fright also manifested itself in the speed at which she worked, which when combined with her lateness further irritated Hawks. *Gentlemen Prefer Blondes* was beginning to run behind schedule, but on a more positive note Hawks realized that it was well worth it. His hunch that Marilyn was a natural for movie comedy was proving to be right.

During the filming of *Gentlemen Prefer Blondes* Marilyn was nominated for an award as "Best Newcomer" by *Photoplay* magazine. The filming of *Gentlemen Prefer Blondes* finished a month after Marilyn's appearance at the *Photoplay* Awards and it had been hard work for everyone involved. Marilyn's nerves had at last been got under control due in part to Jane Russell's encouragement, but mostly it was down to her drama coach, Natasha Lytess. She was on set constantly, arguing with Hawks to allow retake after retake and cajoling Marilyn into improving her performance. Marilyn was also buoyed by the news that *Niagara* had been a major financial success at the box office, grossing four times more than it cost to make. Just a week before *Gentlemen Prefer Blondes* had its premiere, Marilyn and Jane Russell left their handprints and their footprints in soft new wet cement outside Grauman's Chinese Theatre in Hollywood. They both signed their names and above the "i" in Marilyn's name there was a rhinestone to commemorate her new movie; a thief stole it shortly afterwards, and was probably disappointed to find it was not the real thing.

Her latest movie was another in similar territory to her last, although a little more obvious and less subtle. *How to Marry a Millionaire* had commenced filming in March, just four days after she finished filming with Howard Hawks. 20th Century-Fox needed Marilyn in *How to Marry a Millionaire*, despite her tiredness from the demanding schedule she had endured under Hawks. She was big box-office and it was to be one of their first movies filmed in CinemaScope.

During the demanding work with Hawks Marilyn had begun to take Benzedrine tablets, which not only help suppress the appetite but also give you a mild lift. By the end of the movie Marilyn was noticeably slimmer, a condition aided by the hard work of the dance routines. She also seems to have experimented with taking sleeping tablets during the making of *Gentlemen Prefer Blondes*; Nembutal became her usual drug. In September 1953 Grace McKee, Marilyn's old friend, committed suicide by taking drugs; it may have contributed to Marilyn's increased drug taking.

When *Gentlemen Prefer Blondes* had its premiere on July 1, 1953, Marilyn was at a point where she could renegotiate the terms of her 20th Century-Fox contract. For their part they had already increased her weekly salary to $1,250 (worth close to $1 million per year in today's terms). She was also due to leave for Canada to begin filming her next movie (*River of no Return*) but Darryl Zanuck was also trying to get Marilyn's agreement to filming another movie to follow on immediately afterwards: *The Girl in Pink Tights*. Her agent felt that the movie would be a mistake.

"Celebrities and the man in the street crowd Hollywood's famous boulevard to attend the CinemaScope premiere of How to Marry a Millionaire, the first romantic comedy to be filmed in the new miracle medium."

Movietone Newsreel

OPPOSITE: Charles Coburn doesn't look unhappy to be sandwiched between Jane Russell and Marilyn.

"I've got to go to Japan on some baseball business and we could make a honeymoon out of our trip."

Joe DiMaggio proposes
to Marilyn

As proof of her rising star power, when Marilyn clashed with Otto Preminger, the director of *River of No Return*, she was not chastized by Fox, Zanuck, or anyone else.

Back from filming in Canada, shortly before the premiere of *How to Marry a Millionaire* Marilyn made her TV debut when she appeared on *The Jack Benny Show*. It was not her very first appearance on the small screen, as she had made a Royal Triton Oil television commercial in 1950. She then attended the premiere of *How to Marry a Millionaire* with the movie's producer Nunnally Johnson and his wife, and Lauren Bacall and her husband Humphrey Bogart.

Marilyn was still vacillating, along with her agent, as to whether she should do *The Girl in Pink Tights*, a remake of a 1943 Betty Grable movie called *Coney Island*. By mid-December Marilyn was supposed to join Sinatra on the Fox lot to begin filming; she failed to show up for work and after a couple of days it became obvious that she was not going to show at all. She spent Christmas with DiMaggio in San Francisco and by all accounts it was the best Christmas of her life, secure in the DiMaggio family home surrounded by real people who were all relatively normal. Fox, though, had not given up on *The Girl in Pink Tights* and tried to force Marilyn into reporting for work a few days after the New Year. Once again she failed to show up.

Ten days after Marilyn was supposed to be filming at Fox's studio she was dressed in a dark brown coat and walking into San Francisco's City Hall, clutching some white lilies. She was there to marry Joe DiMaggio. Dressed in a blue suit, Joe was already waiting for his bride-to-be, accompanied by the manager of his seafood restaurant on Fisherman's Wharf, his brother Tom and his wife, and an old friend from his days in the minor leagues.

Marilyn signed the marriage certificate as Norma Jeane Mortenson Dougherty. Despite the secrecy surrounding the wedding, there was a sizable crowd of several hundred people outside City Hall when Joe and Marilyn emerged.

From there they headed off on honeymoon to a friend's mountain lodge above Palm Springs, where they spent two weeks. After this they went to Tokyo, via Hawaii. Joe was on baseball business; 20th Century-Fox had little choice but to scrap the idea of *The Girl in Pink Tights*.

Shortly before marrying Joe DiMaggio, Marilyn made a further step toward iconic status when she appeared on the cover of the very first issue of *Playboy* magazine in December 1953. It was not another nude photo shoot for Marilyn: they simply used a picture that had appeared on the infamous calendar taken by Tom Kelly in 1949, along with another taken in Atlantic City when she had offered a photographer a little too much cleavage for DiMaggio's liking.

Following on from her Japan trip with her new husband, Marilyn went to Korea in February 1954 to entertain the troops. She did 10 shows in four days. Back from the Far East, Marilyn returned to Hollywood to rebuild the bridges with 20th Century-Fox, Marilyn and Joe moved in to a rented house on North Palm Drive in Beverly Hills. At the end of April *River of No Return* had its premiere in Denver followed by a first showing in Los Angeles a week later.

OPPOSITE: Marilyn, Bacall, and Grable, photographed by Earl Theisen on the set of *How to Marry a Millionaire*.

Marilyn's new movie was *There's no Business like Show Business*, which began shooting at the end of May; during filming it began to become clear that all was not well between her and Joe. He was the very antithesis of Hollywood and she could just not get to grips with the older man's lifestyle. On the one occasion he attended the Fox lot during filming, DiMaggio, so frustrated with the whole business, refused to be photographed with Marilyn in what he considered a far-too-revealing costume.

It was a matter of days after wrapping up work on *There's no Business like Show Business* that Marilyn flew out of Los Angeles bound for New York's La Guardia airport; Joe DiMaggio was there to send her on her way with a farewell kiss. Marilyn's feet had barely touched the ground before she was filming exterior sequences for *The Seven Year Itch*. One of the shots was the iconic scene of Marilyn in a white dress with her skirt blowing up around her waist while standing over an air duct.

While for us it is an iconic movie moment, it was an apocalyptic event in Marilyn and Joe's relationship. DiMaggio watched it being filmed—it sent his sensibilities over the precipice. The cast and senior crew were all staying in the St. Regis Hotel on East 55th Street in the heart of Manhattan, and no-one in rooms near to those occupied by Mr. and Mrs. DiMaggio got much sleep that night.

A few days later the feuding couple flew home to Hollywood; by the first few days of October it became clear to those close to Marilyn that it was over between her and Joe. Cue the 20th Century-Fox publicity machine to craft a carefully stage-managed announcement that highlighted the fact that their careers were in conflict. Meanwhile Marilyn and Joe stayed together in their rented house at 508 Palm Drive, but on Wednesday morning, October 6, the announcement was made to the phalanx of pressmen waiting outside the couple's Beverly Hill's home. Minutes later DiMaggio sped off in his blue Cadillac and headed home to San Francisco. Marilyn was granted a divorce on October 27, 1954.

The strain of the emotional and professional calls upon her was certainly showing. *There's no Business like Show Business* had its premiere on December 16, 1954, in New York City but Marilyn did not attend. Her entire life was in turmoil—having left Hollywood she had fallen out with not just 20th Century-Fox but she had also fired her agent, Charles Feldman, as well as her lawyer. To clear her head she went to stay with her supportive friends Milton Greene and his wife Amy, at their 18th-century Connecticut farmhouse.

Milton Greene had met Marilyn when she and DiMaggio were in their courting-but-serious phase. A photographer, he was in Hollywood on an assignment for *Look* magazine. He and Marilyn struck up a real friendship and so when she decided to leave Hollywood and strike out on her own it was with Milton and his wife's support and encouragement. After a family Christmas in Connecticut, Marilyn and Milton formed Marilyn Monroe Productions and severed her relationship with 20th Century-Fox. Shortly afterwards, Marilyn moved to a suite in the Waldorf Astoria Towers in Manhattan and lived a lavish lifestyle that was funded by Greene, as she had no money of her own.

"There is nothing else quite like Marilyn on this good earth."

The first issue of *Playboy*

OPPOSITE: Marilyn and Joe DiMaggio leave San Francisco City Hall after their wedding on January 14, 1954. Although they divorced within the year they become good friends and remained fond of each other. DiMaggio reportedly proposed to her again just four days before she died.

Greene worked tirelessly trying to negotiate deals with studios to put a movie into production, and part of this strategy was Marilyn's interview on *Person to Person*, a CBS TV program, broadcast on April 8, 1955. It was filmed at the Greenes' farmhouse with Edward R. Murrow, the broadcaster who had been such an important "voice to America" from London during the early years of World War II. The ten-minute interview showed Marilyn to be eager to please and relaxed with the Greenes.

Shortly before her appearance on *Person to Person* Marilyn met Cheryl Crawford who, along with Elia Kazan, was one of the co-founders of the Actors Studio in 1947 as well as a major Broadway producer. By 1951 Lee Strasberg had taken over the running of the studio. Marilyn told Crawford she was interested in becoming a serious actor and began having private lessons with her. Marilyn soon met Strasberg and his wife Paula and began working at the studio proper; for his part, Strasberg was captivated by what he saw in her.

The Actors Studio had just moved to its current location in what had been the Seventh Associate Presbyterian Church on New York City's West 44th Street, and it was there that Strasberg took over from Crawford and began schooling Marilyn. She would arrive dressed in casual clothes, without make-up, and as one fellow actor said, she appeared to be able to switch her "Monroe character" off and on.

It was while she was going through the Actors Studio's sessions that *The Seven Year Itch* had its premiere in New York on June 1. There was talk of Marilyn and Joe getting back together, but the more time she spent in New York City with the arts crowd, the less likely this became; nevertheless it was DiMaggio who accompanied her to the premiere of *The Seven Year Itch* at Loew's State Theater on her 29th birthday.

In fact Joe DiMaggio would always remain there for Marilyn and never remarried after their divorce. He died on March 8, 1999, in Florida and was interned in Colma, California. DiMaggio last words were "I'll finally get to see Marilyn."

Marilyn was invited to many parties with Lee and Paula Strasberg and others she met at the Actors Studio. At these parties she occasionally bumped into people she knew from her Hollywood days; back in April she had met Arthur Miller again. Shortly after the party he called his friend Paula Strasberg asking if she had a telephone number for Marilyn. Miller arranged to meet Marilyn at the home of Norman Rosten, a poet and old friend from their university days.

ABOVE: After the failure of her marriage, Marilyn moved to New York. Determined to become a serious actress, she took acting workshops at the famous Actors Studio. Here she acts as an usherette at the premiere of James Dean's *East of Eden* donating the proceeds of her services to the Actors Studio.

OPPOSITE: The famous billowing skirt scene was shot on location at Lexington Avenue and 52nd Street. The footage, though filmed, was not used in the finished movie and was later reshot in a studio. This is the emblematic end result that effectively led to the end of her marriage to Joe DiMaggio.

Mrs. Arthur Miller
1956–1959

From the almost frenetic movie-making of the first half of the decade, Marilyn slowed to a snail's pace and turned out just one film a year for the second half, although in 1958 she had no movies released. Marilyn married her second husband, a man as different from her first as it's possible to be. Would she at last find happiness?

"He [Arthur Miller] introduced me to the importance of political freedom in this country."
Marilyn

OPPOSITE: Miller left his wife, Mary, at the beginning of June and within days, on June 29, 1956, married Marilyn in a civil ceremony in White Plains, New York.

Whereas Marilyn's relationship with DiMaggio was carried on in the full, intense white glare of publicity from the day they first met, Marilyn's relationship with Arthur Miller was conducted in near absolute secrecy. Even many of those closest to Marilyn did not know she was seeing Miller in New York.

For Miller, despite having been instantly attracted to Marilyn when they first met in Hollywood in 1951, it was no easy decision to begin the affair. He had married his high school sweetheart in 1940 and the couple had two children, but their marriage, for all sorts of reasons, had got stuck in the doldrums. Nevertheless, Miller, as cerebral as DiMaggio was physical, struggled with his conscience. His work was so important to him and following on from the success of *Death of a Salesman* his play about the Salem witch trials, *The Crucible*, opened in 1953, yet it failed to live up to his, or other people's, expectations. Miller's stance on the McCarthy witch hunt was reflected in *The Crucible* and his failure to testify placed him at odds with the U.S. Government—he was refused a passport in 1954 when he wanted to attend the Belgian opening of the play.

Marilyn was still living in the Waldorf Astoria Towers apartment in Manhattan, and by this time MCA, the influential Hollywood agency, was in discussions with 20th Century-Fox following her suspension by the studio. There were also protracted discussions involving the British playwright Terence Rattigan and the notorious British theatrical entrepreneur Binkie Beaumont over Marilyn appearing in *The Sleeping Prince*. Having not worked for over a year Marilyn certainly needed the money; the production

"Laurence Olivier is said to be 'tickled pink' to be starring in a film with Marilyn."

Daily Mirror, January 1, 1956

OPPOSITE: In 1956 Marilyn starred as wannabe singer Chérie in the movie adaptation of William Inge's Broadway hit drama *Bus Stop* opposite Don Murray as the cowboy, Beauregard "Bo" Decker. Marilyn famously sang "That Old Black Magic" during the movie.

company she formed with Milton Greene had so far been a financial non-starter. As the year ended Marilyn signed once again for 20th Century-Fox, although it was on vastly different terms than her previous contract with the studio. She was only required to make four movies in seven years; through her production company she would receive well over a million dollars in annual salary when measured in today's money. On top of that, Marilyn could make one movie each year for another studio, and she was also guaranteed a share of her movies' profits. In all, she could expect to get somewhere near $100 million (in today's money) for seven years' work.

A day after the deal was inked Fox announced that Marilyn's first movie for Fox was to be *Bus Stop*, directed by Joshua Logan for Marilyn Monroe Productions and 20th Century-Fox. Furthermore, Milton Greene announced that Marilyn was in negotiations to make *The Sleeping Prince* (later filmed as *The Prince and the Showgirl*) after *Bus Stop*, and her co-star was to be Sir Laurence Olivier, Vivian Leigh's husband and one of Britain's foremost actors. On February 9 Marilyn and Larry, as he insisted everyone call him, attended a press conference in New York at which Olivier saw Marilyn-mania at close quarters as photographers jostled each other for prime position. Marilyn, in a low-cut black velvet dress and jacket, had a wardrobe malfunction when the strap of her dress broke, and this very nearly caused a photographers' stampede.

From New York Marilyn flew to Hollywood; it was the first time she had been there since leaving to live on the East Coast the previous year. It was a very different Marilyn from the one that had left. She was now more confident, a better actress, and she had Milton Greene by her side. It had been Greene who had suggested Logan as director of *Bus Stop*, and Logan's only real problem was the fact that Marilyn had hired Paula Strasberg as her acting coach. Strasberg was permanently on set and she was no easy person to get along with. She naturally used the "method acting" approach made famous by Lee Strasberg which some who were working on the movie found ridiculous—this was Hollywood not Broadway.

During the making of *Bus Stop* Marilyn appeared on the cover of *Time* magazine, proof of her collateral as well as wonderful news for Fox and the movie. Everything seemed to be going right for Marilyn, including her love life. Arthur Miller, having separated from his wife, headed to Reno while Marilyn was filming in Hollywood. He stayed there for six weeks in order to qualify under Nevada's arcane laws that allowed for "quickie" divorces. Meanwhile, Marilyn and Miller spoke on the phone every day while he stayed at a guest ranch north of Reno.

As soon as *Bus Stop* was finished in early June, Marilyn went to New York to meet up with Miller who was due to follow a week or so later. Everything was set, both were free to marry and they planned to honeymoon in England so that Marilyn could work with Olivier. However, there was one small problem for Miller: the specter of communism was about to raise its head again.

As Miller was preparing to leave Nevada he was subpoenaed to appear before the House Un-American Activities Committee. Miller had no intention of naming names and he didn't. Ironically, there were those who wanted Marilyn to end her relationship

ABOVE: Filmed in London, *The Prince And The Showgirl* starred Marilyn opposite Laurence Olivier.

with Miller "for the good of her career." Instead she supported him totally. Miller's admission that he was going to marry was the prelude to pandemonium; Marilyn's apartment was put under virtual siege. Over the next few days there was frantic planning by the couple and on June 29 they went before a judge in the Westchester County Court House in White Plains, New York. They were pronounced man and wife at 7:21pm. Two days later they had a Jewish wedding at the house in Katonah, New York before heading to Miller's farmhouse in Roxbury, Connecticut.

Before and after the wedding there was intense behind-the-scenes wrangling over Miller's HUAC appearance. It seemed likely that the House of Representatives would cite Miller for contempt and he would have his passport confiscated. Finally, Miller was given permission to travel.

Marilyn, dressed in a tight sweater and pencil skirt, and Arthur Miller left New York's Idlewild Airport on Friday, July 13, on a Trans World Airlines flight to London so that she could begin shooting *The Prince and the Showgirl*. At London Airport, Laurence Olivier and Vivien Leigh were there to meet them and together they held an impromptu press conference. The following day, the Millers were driven into central London for a more formal press conference at the Savoy Hotel. Marilyn felt that Olivier's aloofness, as she perceived it, was a rebuff, whereas Olivier was simply acting professionally in front of the press; it was the beginning of an uneasy working relationship between the two of them. The situation was not helped by Olivier being none too enamored with Arthur Miller—he disliked his plays and found him smug. Added to which, Olivier was not just Marilyn's co-star he was also her director. It was not long before Miller felt dislike for Olivier.

The first day of test filming went badly, with Marilyn wanting reassurance while Olivier craved professionalism and progress. Nevertheless, when Olivier looked at the first day's rushes he saw why Marilyn was a star—the camera loved her. Rehearsals were due to begin a week later before shooting proper began in August. Before the rehearsals began, Miller heard that Congress had voted overwhelmingly for him to be cited for contempt; it put a damper on their honeymoon and contributed to Marilyn feeling unhappy with just about everything.

Paula Strasberg had come to London with Marilyn, which upset Olivier no end; as filming went on he found it almost intolerable. Also, very early during filming Olivier managed to upset his co-star by asking her to be "sexy Marilyn Monroe." She interpreted this as insinuating that she couldn't act and was some kind of one-dimensional puppet. For his part, all Olivier wanted was to see the woman in the test film.

Miller was busy working on rewrites for *A View from the Bridge* that was to open in October. As Marilyn's anxieties over her movie grew he became increasingly frustrated with his own work. Tensions increased by the day. Olivier had his own off-set issues when Vivien Leigh miscarried their child. Leigh, who was a manic-depressive, sunk into the depths of despair, which naturally reflected on Olivier's ability to remain calm.

Then came the worst blow of all. After a couple of weeks of filming, Marilyn and Miller had a vicious argument; Marilyn was distraught because he would not, unconditionally, take her side against what she saw as the conspiracy against her by everyone who did not work for Marilyn Monroe Productions. The Millers had been married barely two months when Arthur decided to fly home to America. After he had left, Marilyn found out she was pregnant; days later she miscarried. Frustrated in her work, Marilyn took increasingly to drugs, which only made everything worse—even her husband's return didn't help. Back at Pinewood, filming went on but it was a continual drama and it was a miracle that the movie was completed. The Millers left on November 20; their honeymoon had turned into a nightmare, one from which their marriage would never fully recover.

Back from England, they went to Jamaica for a real honeymoon and then moved into an apartment on East 57th Street in Manhattan. All the troubles of England appeared to evaporate and Marilyn seemed blissfully happy with her husband. However, Arthur Miller was not so happy with the arrangements concerning Marilyn Monroe Productions. Miller did not like Milton Greene which sealed his fate; there were even rumors that Greene and Marilyn were lovers. Whatever the truth, Milton Greene was soon eased out of the company.

When *The Prince and the Showgirl* came out in June, to better reviews than anyone who had worked on it imagined possible, the Millers were in Connecticut, but made their way to the New York premiere. What no one knew, apart from their inner circle, was that Marilyn was again pregnant. Two months later she again miscarried. Her earlier happiness ebbed away as she took far too many sleeping tablets and on at least one occasion her stomach had to be pumped to save her life. She was also drinking way too much for her own good, a habit that had grown out of control while filming in England.

Come late July 1958, Marilyn was on her way back to Hollywood. She had been away for two years and the Hollywood press corps was out in force to record her return. She took a suite in the Bel-Air Hotel and returned to work on 4 August with Billy Wilder on *Some Like It Hot*, a movie that was far more befitting her talents. However, it was to prove to be a very mixed blessing.

Billy Wilder needed all his directorial skills to work with Marilyn on *Some Like It Hot*; he also needed stamina as it took five months to complete the picture. Her co-stars were Tony Curtis and Jack Lemmon. Neither her co-stars nor her director could have begun to imagine just how challenging a movie it was going to be—one that has passed into screen legend due to Marilyn's inability to learn her lines. One scene with three words from Marilyn is said to have needed 65 takes. Marilyn was also unwell. Her state of mind needed constant attention from her psychiatrist, who had been flown in from New York. She also went to hospital several times during filming, as she was once again pregnant. Yet again Marilyn suffered a miscarriage.

Marilyn's marriage was more than a little shaky during her work on *Some Like It Hot*. There are reports of Miller joining her in Hollywood but not enjoying the experience one little bit. In an exchange with Billy Wilder, Miller was surprised to learn that Marilyn was not arriving until well after lunch for her first shot, as her director pointed out. She had apparently been leaving their room at the Bel-Air around 7:00am.

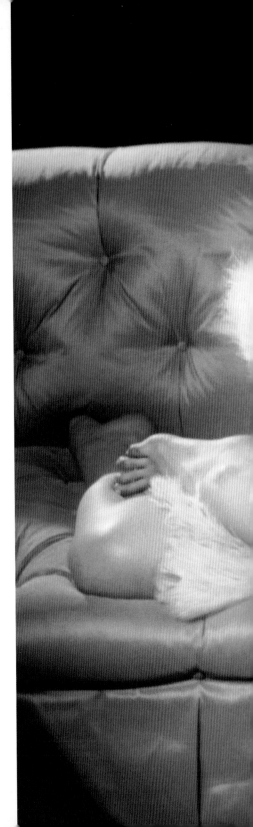

ABOVE: Marilyn pretty in pink for *The Prince and the Showgirl*.

Tony Curtis was married to Janet Leigh when he made *Some Like It Hot*, and shortly after he finished the movie he was asked what it was like to kiss Marilyn. His answer has passed into movie legend: "It was like kissing Hitler." Recently he has said it was a joke. "It was such a darn stupid question, so I gave a stupid answer." He also confirmed that he and Marilyn had an affair some years before making *Some Like It Hot*. He has also said that they rekindled their relationship during its making. What's even more surprising is that they admitted their affair to Arthur Miller in Marilyn's dressing room at the studio on N. Formosa Avenue in Hollywood. "I just stood there. The room was so silent that I could hear tires screeching on Santa Monica Boulevard," said Curtis. Marilyn then told both men that she was pregnant. When Curtis asked Miller what he should do, Marilyn's husband replied. "Finish the film and stay out of our lives." As Marilyn sat there crying, Curtis left her dressing room, walked back to his, and locked the door. It may have accounted for Marilyn's missing mornings.

Shooting on *Some Like It Hot* was completed in November, and soon afterwards Marilyn returned to New York where she entered hospital for some surgery connected with her miscarriages. Their marriage was showing increasing signs of strain. Having got Marilyn away from the temptations of Hollywood and the movie set, Arthur Miller instead became increasingly fed up with what he saw as the undue influence of the Strasbergs. Following the premiere of *Some Like It Hot* in March, Marilyn had gone back to work at the Actors Studio, spending increasing time in the city rather than out at their farm. People have talked of Miller appearing detached from Marilyn, others about how badly she treated him—she the star to Miller's tortured writer.

Given Arthur's brush with Congress and the furor surrounding the HUAC hearings it was perhaps none too surprising that he did not go with Marilyn to Hollywood to meet with the Russian Premier Khrushchev in September 1959. No doubt few in Congress saw any irony in the communist leader visiting 20th Century-Fox's studio for a special showing of their movie musical, *Can-Can*; although Ronald Reagan turned down an invitation to the meet-and-greet. Marilyn decided to wear her tightest, sexiest dress as she considered there probably was not enough sex in Russia.

Spyros Skouras, the head of Fox, introduced Marilyn to the Premier, who had seen a clip from *Some Like It Hot* at an American exhibition in Moscow. "You're a very lovely young lady," said Khrushchev, smiling. Marilyn apparently told him she was married and later revealed that "He looked at me the way a man looks on a woman."

"Marilyn is a kind of ultimate. She is uniquely feminine."
Clark Gable

OPPOSITE: Marilyn and Jack Lemmon in *Some Like It Hot*.

The End
1960–1962

By 1960, Marilyn's lifestyle was not so much hedonistic as almost completely out of control. Her failing marriage, her family history, a career that had become very different from the one that she had hoped for, and the fact that by Hollywood standards she was aging fast, all conspired to create a lethal mix. Soon she would be alone again—it was the thing she feared most.

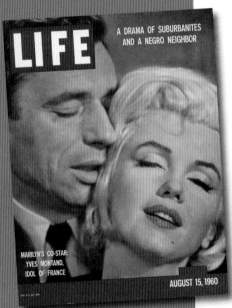

OPPOSITE: Marilyn and Yves Montand had a steamy affair during shooting of *Let's Make Love*.

2 0th Century-Fox was anxious to get Marilyn back to work as she had so far failed to live up to their expectations, with the exception of *Some Like It Hot*, which had done good business in America and was beginning to open around the world. Indeed, a few months later, in March 1960, she won the Golden Globe for Best Actress in Musical or Comedy for her fabulous performance in *Some Like It Hot*. The fact that she had been overlooked for an Oscar was a travesty.

Yves Montand, a 38-year-old French singer and movie star who had been born in Italy, was cast to appear opposite Marilyn in *Let's Make Love*. Montand had appeared in the French movie version of *The Crucible* (1957), and Arthur Miller knew him. Miller very much approved of him playing opposite Marilyn because Montand was a good actor, and also because he and his wife, the actress Simone Signoret, were, to use the phrase popular with the FBI, "fellow-travelers" to the liberal-leaning Miller.

When filming began in January, both the Millers and the Montands stayed at the Beverly Hills Hotel, spending time together socially as well as professionally. Just like many of Marilyn's recent co-stars, Montand found her difficult as well as annoying to work with. As usual, being late on set was Marilyn's *modus operandi*, but there were days when she did not turn up at all. Things got worse when Arthur left. Signoret had also gone home to France, to make a new movie, leaving Marilyn in Hollywood where she

BELOW: Arthur Miller wrote *The Misfits* as a starring vehicle for Marilyn to prove her prowess as an actor.

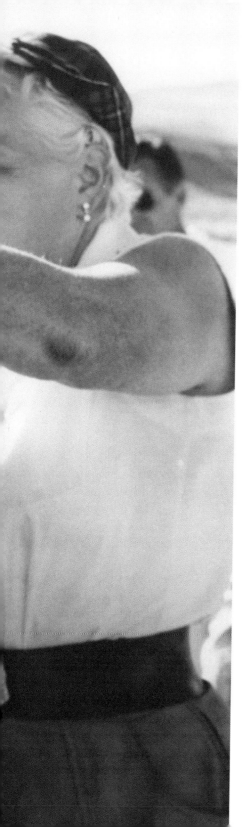

and Montand began an affair. It soon became the stuff of gossip columns. Throughout the making of *Let's Make Love* Marilyn was seeing a new Hollywood psychiatrist. All the signs point to the fact that Marilyn began to feel increasingly adrift during this period, and this was someone who had never felt firmly anchored to anyone or anything. At the same time, Marilyn continued taking prescription drugs that were given to her all too readily by doctors who ought to have known better; in Hollywood there has never been a shortage of such doctors.

As work on *Let's Make Love* was nearing the scheduled date for its completion there was doubt that what Marilyn had shot would be enough to produce a finished movie. When filming finally wrapped up a month later, progress on Marilyn's next movie was gathering pace. Work had started on getting cast and director in place well before *Let's Make Love* had even begun shooting. Her next project was to be the very first movie written by Arthur Miller and was to be produced by United Artists. It was also to reunite Marilyn with John Huston, who had directed *The Asphalt Jungle* ten years earlier and had himself been absent from Hollywood for some years.

"When you look at Marilyn on the screen, you don't want anything bad to happen to her."
Natalie Wood

With the filming of *Let's Make Love* finishing so late, it was just a matter of weeks until work on *The Misfits* was scheduled to begin. Most actors need a time to rest and realign themselves between major roles and with Marilyn's problems, coupled with her drug taking, it was never going to be easy. John Huston, who was unaware of marital difficulties between Arthur and Marilyn, flew into New York from Ireland for meetings with Miller. Meanwhile, Miller was trying desperately to salvage their marriage after Marilyn's unfaithfulness and his feelings of rejection. With just about everyone in Hollywood completely in the know about Marilyn and Montand's affair, it was all so humiliating. There were doubts as to whether it would be possible for *The Misfits* to even begin filming on location in Reno, Nevada.

Naturally Huston heard all about Marilyn and Miller's difficulties as soon as colleagues from Hollywood arrived in Reno. He reassured himself with the fact that as Arthur Miller was comfortable about going ahead with the filming then everything would be fine. His only issue was Marilyn's need to be back in Hollywood in mid-July to do some over-dubbing on *Let's Make Love*. Prior to starting the movie, Marilyn spent two weeks on the East Coast and all concerned hoped that the equilibrium of being back with her husband and at home in Manhattan and Connecticut would help to focus her.

ABOVE: Marilyn and Clark Gable on the set of *The Misfits*. The shoot was arduous for everyone in the extreme desert heat and Marilyn's erratic behavior only made things worse.

A few weeks after Marilyn began work on *The Misfits*, *Let's Make Love* had its premiere. By this time her new co-star was finding their working relationship intolerable. The former "King of Hollywood," Clark Gable, called her "unprofessional" and would get irritated on set waiting for her to show up. For Marilyn it was no longer nerves over her acting that was getting the better of her—it was more booze and more pills. Staying at the Mapes Hotel in Reno she was taking up to 20 barbiturates a day washed down with hard liquor. She was frequently comatose in the mornings.

This was when it became apparent to everyone involved with *The Misfits* that the Millers had little chance of resurrecting their marriage. Marilyn got to the point of ignoring Arthur in front of people on set and, according to Huston, she "embarrassed him." Things were so bad that she again talked of suicide. Filming in the searing heat of the desert was scarcely bearable for all concerned, but it was Marilyn's state of mind that put her close to the edge. One day she took too many pills, maybe deliberately, or maybe because she was too out of it to know what she was doing. After having her stomach pumped she was flown to Los Angeles and spent ten days in the hospital. It was a stay accompanied by the soundtrack of the gossip columnists' typewriters, which did not spare the Millers' dignity. Reporters converged on Nevada to see for themselves what would happen when Marilyn returned to the set.

Miller celebrated his 45th birthday during the making of *The Misfits*, but Marilyn refused to sing "Happy Birthday" during his party. A month later, when they flew home to New York, they did so on separate planes. When they got there, Arthur Miller went straight to a hotel while Marilyn went to their apartment. Their marriage was over.

As was the norm, the press besieged the Millers' apartment building hoping to get a glimpse of Marilyn or, better still, a word from her. She was mostly invisible except for sessions with her psychiatrist, meanwhile every newspaper in America, as well as overseas, was discussing her marriage break-up. With her life becoming increasingly tense, Marilyn told 20th Century-Fox she would not appear in *Goodbye, Charlie* (Debbie Reynolds starred instead) and then immediately after Christmas she went to Mexico for a vacation.

While Marilyn was away on vacation, her lawyer filed for her divorce from Arthur Miller. It was done on the same day as John F. Kennedy was inaugurated as President; it was a good day to bury bad news. Ten days later, Marilyn attended the World Premiere of *The Misfits* at the Granada Theater, Reno on January 31, accompanied by one of her co-stars, Montgomery Clift. Arthur Miller was there too, but they avoided each other.

When the first reviews of *The Misfits* appeared they were overwhelmingly critical, and they singled out Marilyn in particular. It was not what she needed to hear and it was soon after this that she entered a psychiatric hospital in New York. It was Joe DiMaggio who came to her rescue. He persuaded the medics to release Marilyn from the psychiatric hospital and transfer her to another New York hospital.

She was in hospital for three weeks, during which time friends say she grew increasingly listless. Her condition seemed to run soul-deep, and as every day passed so 20th Century-Fox grew increasingly anxious that their star should get back to work

"However confused and difficult she is in real life, for the camera she can do no wrong."

Allan "Whitey" Snyder, Marilyn's make-up artist

LEFT: Marilyn suffered from fragile physical and mental health during filming of *Something's Got To Give*, and out of 33 days when she should have been on set, she only appeared 12 times. She was fired and the movie was cancelled.

ABOVE: Marilyn and Montgomery Clift, were great friends. Marilyn described him as, "The only person I know who is in worse shape than I am." Here they attend the premiere of *The Misfits*, in 1961.

As she got no better, it was DiMaggio who was once again on hand to help. This time he invited Marilyn to Florida. After a couple of weeks Marilyn, feeling much better physically, if not properly recovered mentally, returned to New York, and later flew to Los Angeles to discuss with Fox who was to direct her next movie. While all this was playing itself out, Marilyn spent time in Palm Springs at Frank Sinatra's house. She also went to Las Vegas, where Sinatra was performing at the Sands, and partied with the Rat Pack and other Hollywood glitterati. Among those she met was Rat-Pack original Peter Lawford, who also happened to be married to Pat Kennedy, sister of America's new President.

She moved back to California—a physical shift away from Arthur Miller's world and her marriage. In California she knew she had to work, as she was obligated to 20th Century-Fox to make a movie. She grew ever closer to her psychiatrist, Dr. Ralph Greenson, who, if anyone could, might just be able to dispel the demons and get her mind straightened out. Not that Marilyn was a lot of help to herself, because drink and drugs were still way too prevalent in her life.

Marilyn, despite what seemed like a desire to escape her situation, was all too quick to put herself in trouble's path. Parties were the catalyst and she was regularly seen at the Lawfords' home. One evening in the early fall of 1961 she was invited to dinner at 625 Beach Road, their luxurious Santa Monica home, where the guest of honor was to be Attorney General Robert Kennedy, the President's brother. The night ended with Marilyn drunk and being driven home and put to bed, alone, by Kennedy and an aide.

Two weeks later, Marilyn was given another movie role. It was a remake of a 1939 comedy that Fox was calling *Something's Got to Give*. Because she knew she could not refuse, it brought on yet more depression, not least because it was to be directed by George Cukor with whom she had made *Let's Make Love*. Things became so bad that her psychiatrist put her under round-the-clock care from a team of nurses. There were those close to her that doubted she was really fit enough to be able to complete a movie.

Finally, it seemed that all was ready. Marilyn was due to report for filming in the middle of November and for once Fox were optimistic that she would. But Marilyn failed to show up and her co-star, Dean Martin, was left twiddling his thumbs. Fox yet again suspended her for breach of contract.

It seems that during the previous twelve months an affair of sorts had begun with President Kennedy. Numerous sources have since spoken of it, although it was an infrequent sexual relationship rather than what many would regard as a full-blown affair. Given his position, the security surrounding him, and Marilyn's state of health it had to have been a sporadic relationship at best.

At the same time, or possibly later in 1961, it seems that Marilyn may also have been having sex with Robert Kennedy. It seems this relationship, like that with the President, should not really be called an affair.

Throughout most of this time Marilyn was still seeing her psychiatrist regularly, for periods it was every day. During this period she most definitely went to parties where JFK was in attendance, and not just on the West Coast but also in New York. There

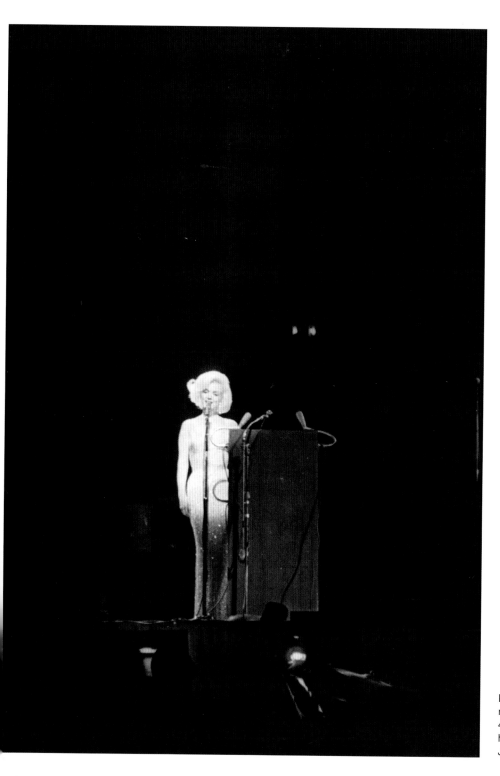

"It's a terrible pity that so much beauty has been lost to us."
John Huston

LEFT AND OVERPAGE: Marilyn gave a sultry rendition of *Happy Birthday* at President JFK's 45th birthday fundraising gala. She wore a figure-hugging flesh-colored gauze dress designed by Jean Louis.

"**She had suffered from psychiatric disturbances for a long time. She experienced severe fears and frequent depressions.**"

A psychiatrist at the inquest
into Marilyn's death

RIGHT: Rear view of Marilyn as she sang her definitive version of "Happy Birthday" at Madison Square Garden for President Kennedy, her sometime lover.

are also those who speculate that during this time she also had a relationship with Frank Sinatra. On top of all that there were ongoing arguments with 20th Century-Fox over the script, casting, cameraman, and just about every other aspect related to the making of *Something's Got to Give*. As 1961 became 1962, Marilyn was getting no nearer to making the movie, but it was inching closer almost imperceptibly.

Finally, something happened to help break the deadlock. Fox suggested that Nunnally Johnson, who was living in Britain at the time, should do some work on the script. He was one writer she trusted as he had written the screenplay for *How to Marry a Millionaire*. Marilyn and her agent knew that time was beginning to work against her. The old adage that in Hollywood you're only as good as your last movie was for Marilyn very true. The failure of *The Misfits*, almost a year ago, was beginning to play on her mind. She badly needed a hit.

In February 1962 Arthur Miller remarried. His new wife, Inge Morath, was the stills photographer who worked on *The Misfits*. Friends of Marilyn have suggested that right up until their wedding she still harbored a fantastic notion that she and Miller could reunite. Marilyn was with Miller's father in Florida when she heard about the wedding. She then spent a few days with Joe DiMaggio before flying to Mexico City and then to Taxco for a vacation, which according to FBI files was arranged by Frank Sinatra. Home from Mexico in early March, Marilyn went to the Golden Globes at the Beverly Hilton Hotel at which she was given a "World Film Favorite" award; her escort was Mexican writer José Bolaños. Marilyn wore a stunning green backless dress and a pair of diamond earrings given to her by Frank Sinatra.

Before March was over, Marilyn went to Palm Desert to a party at Bing Crosby's home. President Kennedy had been due to spend the night at Sinatra's home on Frank Sinatra Drive in Palm Springs; instead, the President went to stay with Bing Crosby in Palm Desert, and Marilyn stayed there too.

FINAL ★★★★
DAILY ☆ NEWS
NEW YORK'S PICTURE NEWSPAPER ®

Vol. 44. No. 36   Copr. 1962 News Syndicate Co. Inc.

New York 17, N.Y., Monday, August 6, 1962★

5¢

WEATHER: Fair.

MARILYN DEAD

Marilyn Monroe: "I was never used to being happy."

(NEWS foto by John Duprey)

THE MONROE SAGA: 7 PAGES OF STORIES AND PICTURES

ABOVE: The Press had a field day after Marilyn's death was made public. The *Daily News* followed the front page with seven pages inside.

Meanwhile, arguments continued over the script. By late April Marilyn had caught a cold and so filming was postponed. Marilyn did finally start work at the very end of April but her attendance at the studio was erratic. The state of her mind was by then teetering on the brink. Dr. Greenson left for a holiday in Europe with his wife. Her support system was shot.

There was barely enough filming going on in May to warrant the term; Marilyn had worked for just one full day. Then to cap it all, Marilyn announced that she was going to New York for a few days, for no other reason than to sing at Madison Square Garden. It was not a concert, but a gala celebration to honor President Kennedy's 45th birthday.

Fox were naturally furious. It was all costing the ailing studio a fortune.

Marilyn left for New York late in the day on Thursday, May 17, and upon arrival she headed for the apartment she still kept in the city. Marilyn was to be the evening's finale. Come Saturday night, her performance of "Happy Birthday" for the President redefined sexy. It was not just her delivery, but the way she acted it out by running her hands all over her body. One columnist described her performance as "making love to the President in full view of America."

"I want to grow old without facelifts. I want to have the courage to be loyal to the face I have made."
Marilyn Monroe

Back at work in Hollywood by the middle of the following week, Marilyn went downhill quickly. 20th Century-Fox were getting ready to fire her. Their relationship was not working and it was costing them a fortune every day she failed to show up for work. A week after Marilyn's 36th birthday, Fox told her she was no longer required for *Something's Got to Give;* they followed it up by suing her for $750,000.

Marilyn's lawyers and her agent desperately tried to salvage the situation but Fox were adamant, and not content with firing Marilyn they suspended the movie altogether. Days later *Life* magazine had Marilyn all over its cover and hinted at the troubles behind the scenes with her movie.

On Saturday, August 4, Ralph Greenson went to see Marilyn during the day. Apart from being upset that her publicist had slept too long, she seemed fine. Pat Newcombe, her publicist, who had stayed the previous night at Marilyn's apartment, left in the early evening, as did Greenson who had a dinner date. Marilyn was upset he couldn't stay, and around 7:30pm she telephoned him while he was shaving to tell him Joe DiMaggio's son had called her. Peter Lawford also called Marilyn, inviting her to dinner, but she declined. Lawford later said her speech was slurred. As the evening wore on there were other calls, including one from José Bolaños (who claimed to be her current lover),

ABOVE: Part of the funeral procession. From back left to front: May Reis, Ralph Roberts, Agnes Flanagan; G. Solotaire; Joe DiMaggio and his son Joe Jr.; Pat and Inez Melson; Rev. F. Darling and Berniece Miracle.

ABOVE: The highlight of Christie's "The Sale of the Century" of Marilyn's possessions was the dress she wore to serenade President Kennedy. The sale realized $13 million, with the dress alone selling for $1.267,500.

OPPOSITE: Flowers on Marilyn's crypt.

who said he thought she sounded fine. Marilyn called a girlfriend at around 10pm and invited her over but she said no, it was too late.

Marilyn, according to the funeral directors, died sometime between 9:30pm and 11:30pm. Her maid, unable to raise her but seeing a light under her locked door, called the police shortly after midnight. She also called Dr. Ralph Greenson who, on arrival, could not break down the bedroom door.

He eventually broke in through French windows and found Marilyn dead in bed. The coroner stated she had died from acute barbiturate poisoning, and it was a "probable suicide."

Once again, Joe DiMaggio stepped into the breach and dealt with much of what needed to be done for Marilyn's funeral. It took place at the Westwood Funeral Chapel on Wednesday, August 8, and Marilyn was placed in a green dress and platinum wig in an open casket. Joe DiMaggio, accompanied by his son, led the mourners. Mostly they were close friends, including Lee Strasberg and Marilyn's publicist, housekeeper, and attorney. DiMaggio excluded everyone from "Hollywood."

Lee Strasberg and Marianne Kris, Marilyn's New York psychiatrist, were left the majority of Marilyn's estate. It was not just her personal items, there was also a substantial amount of money. She had received around $80,000 for her role in *Some Like It Hot* just a matter of weeks before she died. Lee Strasberg's widow, Anna, at a sale in New York in 1999, eventually sold the personal items that Marilyn left to her late husband. It was, with some justification, dubbed the "Sale of the Century."

A pair of jeans worn by Marilyn in *River of No Return* were bought by designer Tommy Hilfiger for $42,550, and the dress worn by Marilyn when she entertained U.S. troops in Korea reached $112,500. Mariah Carey bought Marilyn's white baby grand piano for $662,500, when it had been estimated to sell for $15,000. One of Marilyn's rings sold for $772,500, while one of her Golden Globe awards fetched $184,000. Even 18 necklaces that had been expected to fetch $800 sold for $36,800. The most expensive item was the dress Marilyn wore to sing "Happy Birthday" to President Kennedy—it sold for $1,267,500. The sale certainly lived up to its billing.

In 2005, 200 more items that had belonged to Marilyn were offered for sale by Julien's Auction house in Los Angeles. Yet again, the prices realized were way in excess of the original estimates, even for items of seemingly little value. One of the most intriguing objects was a painting by Marilyn of a symbolic red rose. It is inscribed, "President Kennedy, Happy Birthday and again I say Happy Birthday. Always, Marilyn

Monroe, June 1, 1962." It sold for $78,000 against an estimate of $10,000, which when compared to what had sold at the previous sale seems to be a relative bargain given its double connection. A tan three-ring bound telephone book with the numbers of Marilyn's friends, including Montgomery Clift, Joe DiMaggio, Henry Fonda, Peter Lawford, Jack Lemmon, Arthur Miller, Yves Montand, and Frank Sinatra, sold for a staggering $90,000.

Ironically, everything she had touched was worth more in death than in life. In a way that's exactly what Marilyn has done. She died before she got old and so our memory is of her beauty and her image, a vision that is unsullied by the passage of time. It's not just from the movies and from photographs of Marilyn that we remember her. For every Elvis Presley lookalike and impersonator in the world there are probably two or three Marilyns. Countless events, parties, trade shows, and marketing campaigns have a Marilyn impersonator. Sadly, and of course inevitably, most of them look little like the real thing. Marilyn was a lot more than blonde and red lipstick, yet for most people all they know is that image, the illusion fabricated by Hollywood.

"I knew I belonged to the public and to the world, not because I was talented or even beautiful, but because I had never belonged to anything or anyone else."
Marilyn Monroe

What's on the CD

1. **"Anyone Can See I Love You"** from *Ladies of the Chorus*

2. **"Every Baby Needs a Da Da Daddy"** from *Ladies of the Chorus*
Marilyn's first significant role in movies and her only movie for Columbia, *Ladies of the Chorus* premiered in San Francisco in fall 1948. She sang two numbers, "Every Baby Needs a Da Da Daddy" by Alan Roberts and Lester Lee and "Anyone Can See I Love You" by Irene Cara and Bruce Roberts.

3. **"Kiss"** from *Niagara*
The main reason Marilyn got the part in *Niagara* was that she was younger and cheaper than Darryl Zanuck's first choice, Betty Grable. Choosing Marilyn proved to be a good move as she performed well and on release in February 1953 the film was well received. She sang one song, "Kiss" with music by Lionel Newman and lyrics by Haven Gillespie.

4. **"Two Little Girls from Little Rock"** from *Gentlemen Prefer Blondes*
Fox had a massive hit with this film thanks to the chemistry between the two leads. Among the stand-out songs, beautifully choreographed by Jack Cole, is this adaptation of "A Little Girl from Little Rock" (1949)—music by Ken Darby and Eliot Daniel. It was performed sensationally by Jane Russell and Marilyn.

5. **"When Love Goes Wrong, Nothing Goes Right"** from *Gentlemen Prefer Blondes*
With music by Hoagy Carmichael and lyrics by Harold Adamson, this was one of the songs written specially for the film and did not come from the original 1949 stage musical.

6. **"Diamonds are a Girl's Best Friend"** from *Gentlemen Prefer Blondes*
Marilyn's solo in the film became her signature tune. She did most of her own singing, with the exception of a few high notes at the beginning of the song that were sung by Gloria Wood. It was written by Jule Styne and Leo Robin for the original stage musical.

7. **"Bye Bye Baby"** from *Gentlemen Prefer Blondes*
Another song by Leo Robin (lyrics) and Jule Styne that came to the film from the stage musical. The film became the ninth best box-office seller for the year after release in July 1953.

8. **"One Silver Dollar"** from *River of No Return*

9. **"River Of No Return"** from *River of No Return*

10. **"Down in the Meadow"** from *River of No Return*
A thin western, that owes more to its CinemaScope images of Banff and Jasper National Parks than its story, saw Marilyn cast as a dance hall singer. In a captivating outfit, she sings three songs with lyrics by Ken Darby and music by Lionel Newman.

11. **"After You Get What You Want, You Don't Want It"** from *There's no Business like Show Business*

12. **"Heatwave"** from *There's no Business like Show Business*

13. **"Lazy"** from *There's no Business like Show Business*
Irving Berlin provided the songs for *There's no Business like Show Business* and the music was by Alfred and Lionel, Newman, Earle Hagen, Bernard Mayers, Hal Schaefer, and Herbert Spencer. Marilyn wore Travilla costumes for the film and her dance moves—again choreographed by Jack Cole—were controversial, in particular the torrid "Heat Wave" which she performed with a number of male dancers.

14. **"That Old Black Magic"** from *Bus Stop*
First recorded and released as a single by Glenn Miller and His Orchestra, with music by Harold Arlen and lyrics by Johnny Mercer, this was the only song in the film Marilyn chose as her first solo outing for Marilyn Monroe Productions. The movie earned Marilyn some great reviews when it was released at the end of August 1956.

15. **"I Wanna Be Loved By You"** from *Some Like It Hot*
Bert Kalmar, Herbert Stothart, and Harry Ruby wrote one of Marilyn's most loved songs for one of her most loved films. Regularly voted in the top ten comedies of all time, it is helped by wonderful performances by the principles, although Marilyn's iconic role didn't even win her an Oscar nomination.

16. **"Running Wild"** from *Some Like It Hot*
As Sugar Kane, the singer for Sweet Sue's Society Syncopators, Marilyn was funny, sexy, and played the part to perfection. She performs "Runnin' Wild" by A.H. Gibbs, Joe Grey, and Leo Wood during a memorable scene on the train taking the band to California.

17. **"Some Like It Hot"** from *Some Like It Hot*
Written by Matty Malneck and I.A.L. Diamond, the *New York Times Review* summed up Marilyn's performance as "the epitome of a dumb blonde and a talented comedienne."

18. **"Let's Make Love"** from *Let's Make Love*
The film received a nomination for an Academy Award for Best Original Music Score for Lionel Newman and Earle H. Hagen. It included a number of songs—the title track included—written by Jimmy Van Heusen and Sammy Cahn.

19. **"I'm Through With Love"** from *Some Like it Hot*
Written by Gus Kahn, Matty Malneck, Joseph A. Livingston.

20. **"My Heart Belongs To Daddy"** from *Let's Make Love*
Cole Porter's classic was written for the 1938 musical *Leave It to Me!* He probably would not have expected to see it performed as part of a stunning pole-dance routine by a leotard-clad Marilyn at her most captivating!

Index